elvis presley

is alive and well

and living in harlem

elvis presley

is alive and well

and living in harlem

Elvis Presley is Alive and Well
And Living in Harlem

by Brian Gilmore

THIRD WORLD PRESS
CHICAGO, IL.

First edition 1992
First printing 1992
ISBN: 0-88378-004-6
LC#: 91-65914

Manufactured in the United States of America
Third World Press
7524 S. Cottage Grove Avenue
Chicago, IL 60619

Dedication

This poetry collection is dedicated to Daphne Anita Powell who shared her poetry with me. It was she who inspired me to share my own poetry with the world.

Special Thanks

Of course, first and foremost, to my family for their never ending support, to Junette Pinkney (for friendship), Peter Harris (for being an elder poet-friend), E. Ethelbert Miller (for always having time), to Haki Madhubuti (for a chance), Marita Golden (for making me dare to try), and to Pansye Atkinson (for forcing me to write about the things that matter). God Bless All . . .

contents

I. bo diddley's guitar
reminds me
of . . .

Angry Voices

I. RAY (The Faithful)

plastic eye patches shade the eyes of the prince
bitterness surrounds his kingdom
a pale haze bleaches and concentrates
exiling the faithful to
second class enjoyment.

his smoking jacket glistens,
his stony fingers tap,
his countenance wavers
and senses
the absence of his soul.

he halts and sways no more: he can see
                             he can feel

his protest is deliberate,
his pausing, a defiance
his anger — consistent
his voice hails an eerie silence:
no georgias,
no right times,
no tears to drown in

he won't be driving this bus,
its destination undignified,
its fare unbalanced.

he turns and stumbles,
walks off unassisted,
vanishes
as his valet wipes the tears
that have dripped on his stool.

II. SAM (The Brave)

cockiness bleeds
it is a thoughtless gall,
harboring frustrations
of many years past.

its pinnacle is a singer
his torso frantic,
mooning rec execs
outside club walls.

blackness is anger
making lobbies in a lobby
demanding "unearned privileges"
nobodies have earned,

like,
signing at the desk,
or phoning for champagne,
feeling soft embroidered towels
after a nice steamy bath.

"TREAT HIM LIKE A MAN!"
or at least like,
most singers,
who have come to rest
after the wailing
at the club
is over for the night.

III. BO (The Exploited)

bo diddley's guitar reminds me of the
theory of land enclosure
screaming out heritage in those places
where we should rule.

it is a steamy brothel in miami,
rich acres in meroe,
fingers riveting in motion
trying to guarantee a crumb

yea, that guitar...
its squareness,
the puppetry of councils.
its redness,
the color of ink.
the tune it plays,
an ode to mr. chess.

it plays facades serenading
dotted lines,
hums stories about
unclaimed beauties,
recites anger at
rock and roll galas.

bo's guitar bellows an
unfulfilled dream,
a chart hit where
the singer can't sing,
a raided tract naked
of all it had to offer.

its strings are broken
used to tie us down tight,
linking realities of now

with realities of then,
causing grown men to cry
while singing the blues.

IV. MEMPHIS (The Stolen)

"say chuck, ain't dat dat guy elvis in the back?
clutchin' his gee-tar and a tape recorda' too?"

"sho-nuff, bet e'll 'av a hit next week?.
happens all the time. he deserve it tho,
any wite boy wit' dat much nerve,
to come in 'ere wit' that recorda' 'n all,
rite in front of all these spades,
wit' all this hate,
wit' all this energy jus' ready to explode,
has gotta be a king."

"sho nuff, mr berry."

elvis

1.

elvis presley is alive and well
and the world scrapes near the ground

at the north pole, a flag remains unplanted
in egypt, there are no pyramids.

elvis presley is alive and well
but there is no such thing as superman,
> *there was never a thing called slavery*
> *there was never a rape of africa.*

elvis presley can beat jesse owens
because jesse never ran a race
> *bob gibson is throwing knuckleballs*
> *kareem is shooting jumpers.*

elvis presley is alive and well and i swear i
saw him in harlem
> everyone bolt your doors!
> everyone board up your windows!!
> everyone stop taking singing lessons!!!
> no one is writing this down!!!!

elvis presley was a black man
and al jolson didn't need any make up,

> for it is proven
> and i believe it to be true

> elvis taught bruce lee karate!

7

2.

elvis shouldn't have been allowed
to
register
and vote

3.

shoot him with fire hoses

4.

such a mass,
such a disturbing mass. such a wallowing in the mud
mass   such a dangerous mass.

couldn't live up to it,
couldn't be it, ain't that great,
ain't that bad, ain't that cool.

the mass didn't make up those moves, didn't make up
that voice, those clothes, those ways of crooning
and swaying and fooling the world with that whole
weird way of doing things.

they bought it. swallowed it. bathed in it.
ate it   with a gin and tonic but shit,
hold the tonic because i don't understand it,
i can't face it unless my head is spinning!

the mass couldn't do it all because mud is like
blood;   mud is about emotional outrage!
the mass could never be it all because
america is an illusion and for those of us
watching
tv
all the time — iranians don't care about some white
boy acting like a nigger snorting velcro.

that goes the same for the middle east
and asia
and afghanistan
and afrika
and most of the
world.

but now you're saying — 'japan loves elvis,
seen those impersonators...'

but japan ain't been japan since 1945;
japan is manhattan or chicago or london

damn sure ain't japan!

you're saying the same about other
countries too who are into it
long after we were into it

but really they aren't into it
because once you are into it
you can't call yourself an
afrikan or

an asian
or an arabian.
call yourself whatever you want,
but don't upset the ancestors,
they know about the mud and that
emotional outrage.

still there is that mass.

that huge monster looming over us larger than life
a wailing soul simulating bantu and yoruba wearing
zoot suits and breaking more black sisters' hearts
than chuck berry could mend with 'maybelline' or
'thirty days.'

so the mass swelled and got muddy. the mass got so
big and muddy it couldn't see or walk, realized it
couldn't be superman
couldn't be the lone ranger
couldn't be captain america throwing his mighty
shield.

the mass knew different.
knew about chitlins, whiskey
and juke joints.
knew he stuck out like a sore thumb.
knew he didn't make it because he was better than
anyone
else
because memphis had 500 young white boys around
1950 whose old man or grandmother bought them a
guitar and some ray charles' records for christmas.

he just knew better than the rest that velcro was a
magic potion.
and magic makes people snort velcro.
and snorting velcro makes people wallow in the mud at
night.

and mud makes us look like something we aren't.
because
the mass wasn't white,
he had too much mud in his hair
and snorted too much velcro.

and the mass wasn't black because
he had too much velcro in his hair
and not enough mud hanging off his lips.

the mass was just dangling on a vine holding a
guitar
and some watermelon wondering

why did he want to be what he truly despised?

5.

sick the dogs on him!!

6.

where the hell is bull connor?

7.

elvis lovvvvvvvvvveeeeesssss

pig knuckles.

mystical (for peter tosh)

legalize the thoughts of the
mystic man,
taste his angered daggers.
here his gun rifles
scream torpedo into veracity,
watch his locks flame strength
into purpose.
hate him. loathe him.
despise him.

       love him.

look for him on the frontline.
his words are right centered
afrikan.
he bites,
hails,
shouts,
he gamely accuses and takes
his lumps.

his guitar blades the wind.
his drums decree war with
the world.
what gallish spite!
courage!
wrecker!
"steppin' razor!"
rasta!
dread!
bush doctor!
prophet!
warrior!
pure kemite.

mali male exacto,
tasting,
demanding,
doing what is necessary
saying what is essential.
bringing on thoughts buried
in mental graveyards,
living beside walls of warfare
                              unafraid.

into the void,
the insanity,
the fire,
screaming,
yelling,
accepting no concessions,
never denying to be
100% afrikan
rude boy...

bleeding,
beaten,
bruised,
bludgeoned,
beguiled.

unyielding blackness.
eternal free man living
on through departure and
meeting the needs
of his people's mission —

tosh lives,

                    he lives!
lives
lives

lives
lives
lives

light a candle for peter
and
hum
forever...

       fight on.

september is not change

it is september now

the month has changed but south africa
remains the same

in september leaves fall
from trees like the dead
children don't wait until
december to be seen naked

the breeze blows hard when
trucks come through the townships
they do not come to clean
leaves off the street

september is not change

the september papers read like
august papers
july papers
june papers
headlines of blood and fire
burning ash between my fingers

in september i pray for jesus
i pray for mohammed
i pray for someone
somewhere to make september
not like all the other months

in september
children return to school
after summer vacation
and count missing friends

they haven't been to any funerals
and no one has moved

it gets cold in september
and the daylight of our communities
dies into darkness earlier

in johannesburg it has always been cold
and the darkness they breathe growls
into tomorrow like wolves on the hunt

we "beach" it on labor day
inhaling seagulled dew of peaceful fantasies

in soweto they prepare for labor strikes
called "shoot 'em down"

animals collect nuts and
wild fruit and prepare hideaways
for winter
soweto has always been a hideaway
for the brave and for those who dare
say "change"

september is not change

september swells of pine and oak
and my nose itches from ragweed

south african noses burn the
smoke of dutch guns
and tear gas shot off the night before
while we slept

the cold rainstorms of september blow
down the wooden tenements in south africa
and we complain about muddy shoes on our
carpets

the disfigured shack neighborhoods
have no orange brown trees for shade
and we scream laziness about raking
up "beauty" on saturday mornings

september is not change

they say october is full of
mystery and suprises
in south africa the mystery
has unfolded and there are no
surprises coming
until the men
stop

falling
to

the
ground

like
leaves.

conversation and carob cookies

there is so much to say,
sit,
have a carob cookie and sit.
where have you been?
listen.
don't u.s. warships have radios?
sit,
have another cookie.
sit,
it's pronounced "a - part - tide"
and it's been going on for decades,
cookie,
no, i don't agree with reagan or thatcher
sit.
sit down and learn biko
cookie,
no, i don't drink beer and i hate navy shirts
because biko was just as bad as malcolm,
sit,
soweto.
cookie,
didn't they have a radio on your ship?
cookie,
people are dying everyday in soweto   soweto -
repeat...   people are dying everyday
in soweto!
cookie,
apartheid,
if idi amin were president and if all the suburbs
were indian reservations, you wouldn't have asked
me that and you wouldn't be wearing a navy shirt,
sit,
you would be asking me for more cookies,
sit,
no, beer doesn't go well with carob drop cookies,

sit,
mandela.
sit.
three more cookies,
martin luther king was a king,
so was malcolm,
america taught south africa that
mandela is a king,
cookie,
selma was a made for tv movie but soweto
broke the cameras,
sit,
luck don't strike twice and the the 80's will never be
the 60's because people learn from the mistakes
of others,
sit,
especially the dutch,
sit,
i have more cookies,
sit,
tutu.
tutu is a king without a constitution,
and his nobel is a raven,
sit,
it doesn't matter that you didn't know
it only matters now that you do,
sit,
tell your buddies that you hate carob cookies,
sit,
but you ate them anyway,

exit.

there is more than one burundi

it is camouflage
the same rotted meat
the same egg plant infested with crickets and
cicadas
the same story i've grown to hate

the papers say,
here is injustice
here is legitimate irrefutable evidence
of afrikan ignorance and inhumanity
here is proof

but surfaces have insides
california has san andreas

burundi is a larger picture,
                    a boil,
answers trapped inside a
pulsating trickle of confusing interiors

interiors, remember that word — interiors.

burundi is projection,
            old projections,
so old one would think it was obvious
yet so casual our pockets say:

          "it is what it is," —

     accept those surfaces people,
     smoother roads are paved everyday.

look inside these burundis,
look inside with microscopes,
                    delicate sense,

closed eyes,
open minds,
burundis are volcanoes,
you wouldn't blame lava unless
it burned your arm.

burundis are surfaces DAMMIT:
burundi is philly
motown
chocolate city

they are all burundi
supercharged relocations with
puppets playing house,
well designed mayhem fashioned
to maintain belligerence

burundi -
hindus and muslims in india
south african majorities
haitian nightmares
salvadorean skepticals
nicaraguan disharmony

and theories saying,

it is easier to listen to
dan rather than it is
to

identify earthquakes.

upon becoming black

cliff tried to warn us.
it was a camp director's duty,
our mommas would have slapped
him if he hadn't,

we were young.

the beach air was fresh,
smelled like
perfumed feathers
of a rare bird,
banishing distant thoughts
of concrete jungles.

the beach was white:

sand.
clouds.
salt.

people.

cliff tried to warn us,
we were young.

he told us they would
look at us,
they would stare,
they would send messages
without uttering the slighest
word.
he told us about the water where
we could swim and play free,

where we wouldn't have to worry
as much about those frowns
and those thousands of eyes calling

us

monkey.

on the boardwalk the storekeepers set us
straight from the start,
felonious frowns from civil war cinema,
confederate tales tacked in time,
antebellum anger arranged and
arrogant.

we didn't want trouble
didn't even want to buy anything,
just wanted to be like
everyone else,
but we weren't everyone else,
we were dr king's kids,
we came to start trouble,
we were all the same
it was said.

we tried every store,
they were all the same,

1960 and selma is a beach,
1860 and maybe i would
have laughed,

so we went to swim like cliff said,
talked about the white beach
and white sand,
about storekeepers with
broomsticks and telephones
ready,

and how everything would be different
from this day forth because we were
no longer innocent and no longer
young.

only three blacks

In management class,
they want us to be a
clearly defined

entity

of shameful deficiency,

because the only miss america
that we ever remember is named

vanessa

therefore, to conceal
inadequacies —
whether intended or not —
group projects in class
become segregated
by "inclusion,"

those of us left over,
have to hold a press conference.

winter's revolution

we have been
here
       so long
been
here
so long
         been
         here
         for
         such
    a long long
         time

we should be hockey players
by now.
no
more
      cold
      weather
excuses
      pro
      slavery
excuses
      anti
      progress
excuses
no more talk
about
strangers
in a strange land
we are
in the place
where we are supposed
to be fighting   why else are jamaicans
into bobsledding now
they are   with us.

we have been here so long been here so long
been here for such a long long time
that i get excited by the cold
because
we
know
how
to
        build
        fires
and
store
        food
we
have
learned
the basics

        the
        wilderness
        is
        vulnerable
    this time of
year

just like

they

split up
        afrika
when
it

was

a hundred and six.

we
have
      been
      here
      so
      long
been
here
so
long
      been
      here
and
become
part
      eskimo
chicago
is
like
siberia

haki and gwen live
in
chicago

june jordan is from
ny
and
ny
reminds me of

      antarctica

there are some bad poets in cleveland
who read langston while ice skating

so
what if our women will have to
dress
like
russian women
so what if
we will have to
    learn to ski

this
is
good.

we have been here for
so long been here so long
been
here for such a long long time that
sometimes when
i think
about all those
snowball fights
and all that
wild and dangerous sleigh
riding
i know being a kid
was
good for something
because it's not getting any warmer
we will not leave america
and
the dab of mulatto blood
i borrowed
from europe
has just been sitting   waiting
and
            just chillin'.

YOUTH GARDENS

reap and sow

let
the gardens
grow
tall,
green
youth
fresh
piercing
sun daisy,
cleanse
high
tulip,
azalea
young
weeds,
planted
spring
root,
worlds being made

let
the gardens
be
watered
soil
rich
rose,

rise,

rise,

beanstalk
balmy,

let
the gardens
bloom
nuance,
sprawled
on the
vines,
wet
clear
nurtured,
rising
towards
the heavens.

african violets

rainforest
our
violets,
shield
them
with
our oak,

droop
down
our
leaves,
block
all
the storms,

hang
on
their
limbs
thoughts
sprinkling
pepper,
tend
with
gentle strength,
sacrifical
twigs.

jades

show
the jade
how
to dream,
let
it build
in the
air
skies
of
hope
and green
thick
leaves
of power
and

purpose,
let
the jade
be
a
brick,
stems
of
firm
steel
smelted
to life
with
loftiness,
tender
lovin'
care
fermented
in
a
flora
of
men.

forbidden

WHO PLANTED COCA
POPPY AND CANNABIS NEXT TO MY VIOLETS AND
MY JADES?!!!!! WHO TRIED TO VULTURE
THEM WITH CRICKETS?!!!!!
WHO IS RESPONSIBLE FOR THIS DRY
WOOD AND LUMBER?!!!!!

LET MY SHOVEL BE AN AXE
LET THE RAIN DROWN
THEM ALL THE WAY TO
THEIR ROOTS!
LET THEIR SOIL ERODE!

forest

positive
branches
of
focused
forest,
farmlands
perspecting
into
quagmires
of algae,
waterspout
lovely
the
gardens
of youth,
in
the
wind they blow
always
progressing.

seeds

let
the seeds
of our
children
fall
freely
into
soils
of generations,

seeping
knowledge
into
moss,
building
stems
of
tomorrow,
youth
gardens
will
be
infinite
with
directions
of
joy,
mothers
of
harvest
forever
into
time.

she was a painting (...and i wished to be an artist)

i could wildly kiss her
remove her lipstick
wipe off her clothes

or

wipe off her lipstick
remove her clothes
wildly kiss her

it doesn't matter
only her face on my canvas
"still lifed"
and water based

soon she shall
be hanging in my
bedroom
i can see
exotic colors
on strokes of my brush

　　lightly re-creating
　　details of
　　brown
　　skin

　　lightly re-creating
　　afrikan nudity with
　　bold emotions

　　　　soft hands...

gentle feet...

passionate   places . . .

i paint nudes slow and deliberate because heat
in my house works best when needed most

i paint nudes best because you only see chill
bumps when you are close to someone

i paint nudes life-like because i never was
good at faking orgasms

i painted this nude because

i could wildly kiss her
remove her lipstick
wipe off her clothes

or...

slave ship ride

the oak prison rocks tight,
bouncing briskly towards the
white land

wood puddles sweat
on the shiny black bronze:

> black lips
> black legs
> black knees

black all over!

mahogany pillars separate the captured
friction of these "houses in motion,"

> houses searching for the best
> position during the middle passage.

the passage is steamy,

> hot,

the passage is arched back aching,

> shuddered limb weak,

the passage is damp,
> constantly damp,
walls wetting profusely with
wailings of togetherness
as we arrived in the white land
exhausted and still shackled together.

cybelle by the pool

a. i see her

i see her,
southern tall belle sashaying hips
locks of softness bareback,
swimming cloth cling hiding nature's gifts
she walks whistling lily.

on her toes
she prances gazelle
high aloft my countenance
lemon pure skin dripping
wet with want,
she swiftly stares sunlight.

eye to eye i encounter and focus,
exquisite avenues of beauty
she commands her turf
stirring my core,
sunflower sweet and steamy.

b. **watching her swim**

bouncing;

knees impeccable,
legs ready,
heels and ankles saying,

touch me.

desire to dive where
water awaits,
gyrations reminding me of,

an envelope.

turns of tea
cranberry cove,
mellow lust simmers,
hot flame kicks.

cool down floating,
the water wants more,
she dog paddles chest heaves
i never forget.

c.   after the swim

dried off and semi-dressed
this is unbelievable,
her island charms compel me to talk,
i,
a man of few words.
chrysanthemum mist sealed
in clover balm shorts,
i remember when she approached,
leotard mangos and curves of cream,
my eyes were locked in on
zipper.

d.   we talk

blacker than me
although lighter,
i discover confidence i wish i had,
intelligence which pulls me close,
and a posture indignant with passion.

the sound of her voice
is the beat of my heart,
i imagine a kiss for an hour,
the grass she sits on
is pure and clean,
maybe i can take it home.

e.   the movies

we sat in the theatre,
sharing goobers and rasinets,
she sipped a carbonate urge,

an accident occurred:

                        her hand brushed mine,

my thoughts grew happy.

thought about —
rings and fingers, crowded churches full of
family and friends.
thought about —
entwined fingers, satin sheets, and sweaty
faces lit by night light.
then our legs brushed lightly,
i went to the bathroom.

f.   gone

she vanished,
on a florida avenue one-way,
destination: forever.

she left me memories of wetness,
of elegance,
of walks engulfed in nirvana.

that's all i have,
all i ever will have,
no photos,
no phone numbers,
no letters to read.
though each time i swim
i can see her in the clear lucid
freshness,
her soft face shining,
her ankles gleaming,
her kissable toes splashing,

and that lemon skin,
i can just about taste it.

leave this to the bigots

get a novel published the easy way
same way they sell newspapers
or win
elections
same way they pass laws
and pretend it is
reconstruction,

like those theories
they expound —

smaller brains.
monkey origins.
blacks are really white.
egypt is in
europe.

male bashing.

black males.

black-mail sister!!

novels,

not written by
conservative scholars
or
william styron,
not written
by negroes or
some neo-nazi journalist,

novels by black women buried
under heavy stomping boots,
novels threatened with empty pages
and a life of listlessness,
novels precise in their bloodied ink,

and most of all,

novels under duress
because a true "sister"
knows...

her audience is not the
captive

spirituals (for pansye)

sister gospel truth with the robust voice
sing your song sister,
sing it out real loud,

let us learn it and be strong
as you exhale your sermon of
ceremonial remembrances
and poignant questions:

who shall we love?
who shall we depend on?
who shall we fight for?

sing it sister,

make my day boil with truth,
my nights echo with anger,
my mornings awaken with struggle.

and sister,
whey you finally grow weary,
when your voice tires from ancient yearnings,
no worry,
africa shall rise
with a choir of your children
leading the world in your spirituals.

this macho thing

forget about fish & oceans, forget about
camels & deserts, forget about who & why
& who said what.

forget about being strong,
forget about men don't cry & this thing about
lookin' like a chump in front of the fellas,
cuz' the fellas been crying out for years
to care for somebody.

forget about macho
cuz' macho ain't never prevented suicide,

& forget about just forget about it,
cuz' that's just it, i
couldn't forget about it

couldn't forget about
all those instances,
all those dreams,
all those hand holdin' walks under bright
yellow moons
couldn't forget about places,
and songs
both special and sad
couldn't forget about frozen frames
of unblemished memory.

don't wanna be strong anymore
don't wanna be macho anymore
don't wanna have to forget about anything,
just wanna be able to
cry like everybody else,

just wanna be a man.

the dancer (for d.p.)

i.   the club

blue light sexy
precious precious love,
let the satin soft curtain
call you to my eyes,

float high heeled ebony
white laced crisp,

soar high wire sleek
on a thread of chanel.

what do i call lips of lime?

what do i call skin of silk

what do i call hips of mink?

you know how to dance,
you know how to walk.

ii.   dark rose

you are a rose petal,
may i rescue you from your
hidden bush?
feel the softness
of nature's fluffy fuzz?
strawberry color my heart
with spice?
plant you home and water you

moist?
or snip your stems and kidnap
your roots?

iii.   afrika

ain't afrika great,
sculpturing you with nubian
stone,
tinting you proud
with rivers black,
and legs like columns from
timbuktu.

afrika sweet
apple berry drip
cocoaed flesh
glazed in gem,
afrika strut
afrika sway
rhythmic moves of mali grace,
rise bright dance in
nature's garb,
wrap me in fashion
dark and wet.

iv.   rhythm

dance baby!
teach me how to juju,
teach me hips with sockets
hands of magic
fingers exploring my quivering belly,
purr close to my nose
between wiggling ears,
knees entwined
in a gorge of us,
lips as one
chewing heat,
all night long the drums are heard,
the glowing moon of afrika we,
songhay screams
lost in our shouts.

v.   love roots

the dancer dances smoothly
on my back,
light and airy
the touch of twig,
forever is a tree
growing out of my heart.

II. richard wright is the consummate alien

We must not be cows

I've always hated wiggly lines:
wiggly lines on my TV set
making the picture impossible to comprehend;

my doctor says —
                    this can ruin your eyes
                    this is unhealthy.

Wiggly lines irritate my wisdom teeth,
make them swell and start cuttin',
I am watching news and eating chocolate
forgetting about next week's check-up.

I ate a steak last night,
there was a little TV set on the
fatback,
wiggly lines splintering a newscaster's
face who thinks afrika is really a

        "COUNTRY":

        Nigeria must be NY.
        Mozambique is Florida.
        Egypt is Michigan.
        Rwanda is Rhode Island.

I sleep hard at night   dream of wiggly lines
that wiggle,
I eat jigsaw puzzles while reading Koran,
shatter dishes   scan the Bible,
when I wake I toss my television with the sliced up
newscaster out the window,

He still talks of country
still makes my tooth ache

    still
makes

my

      sirloin   taste

strangely   like

    h

       a   m

  b   u

  r   g

  e

      r.

bigot poem

in between
sit-cons
and the
wheel of misfortune

they sell all
                    types
   of   stereos

because last night
i saw a cracker eating watermelon
a jap selling crack
a jew on a heat grate
and a nigger in a limo

gEOGRAPHy

A mAp Is NoT cLaY
sQuAsHeD aNd MuShEd
InTo PiRaCy AnD fAlSeHoOd

MaPs MeAn MuCh In OuR
fLaT wHiTe WoRlDs Of
MeRcAtOrIaN mAlevOlEnCe

ReAl MaPs LoOm
In FrOnT oF
lIttTlE

bLaCk
EyEs

AnD tElL
pSyChiC pHeNoMeNoN
lIkE
dId YoU kNoW tHaT
tHeRe ArE mOrE nIgGaS
oN eArTh ThAn CrAcKeRs
AnD tHaT

aMeRiCa Is A

        pImPlE

                (mApS hIsToRiCaLly
                HaVe BeEn DeAlInG
                lOsT tRaVeLeRs
                HeAvY bLoWs WhEn
                ThEy DoN't GiVe

                PrOpEr DiReCtIoNs)

ThE nEw MaP
iS aN eVeR

e X p A n D i N g

S

u

D

a

N

e

S

e

T r I b E s M a N

wHo PlAyS bAlL iN tHe StAtEs AnD sWeArS aFrIkA aIn'T
eVeR lOoK tHaT wAy WhEn He LiVeD tHeRe

NoT fAt AnD
sHoRt LiKe
A bUrGeR
eAtInG eXeCuTiVe

BuT talL aNd SpAcIoUs
LiKe

KaReEm*

WiTh HiS

a R m S

s P r E a D o U t

Kareem Abdul Jabbar - Recently retired basketball star of the National Basketball Association. Leading scorer in its history. Approx. height: 7 ft, 3 in.

horror movie

stop counting spooks...

...this addition   and   subtraction
of
                    abnormality
                    is
                    insignificant.

we have plenty of ghosts
                    in
the dc govt but the   schools
still
tell you that
the   first slave
couldn't
                             count to 10.
in atlanta
the   govt is haunted
but nobody in   washington
                             is afraid,
and philly
has some   real   scary   werewolf
                             types
who think
raw
meat
smoldering with a taste of
brick is   GOODddddddddddd.
around inaguration time we

                    count spooks

                    "carefully"

59

                    and accuse wildly if
one
                        frankenstein monster
if one frankenstein creation with a brain that's
been dropped on concrete and juggled around
like jell - o

doesn't get a chance

to fight the wolfman or the mummy or the invisible
men.

but remember igor,   "mastah…mastah…
                              it's time."
            — sound familiar?

now the cowardly lion had something:

"i do believe in spooks, i do believe in
spooks, i do i do i do believe in spooks,"

damn that lion, he should have been a scarecrow

because
frankenstein
was
not a
man
and
i never have been afraid of the dark.

useless pygmalion

bantu and zulu dancing
exquisitely to
mike j
and whitney h
eating deep deep deep
fried chicken cooked in
funny little huts by
guys named popeye
and the colonial

the new black man has
a life long subscription
to jet and ebony
and seems to always give
his paycheck to
the united negro college fund
naacp
and traditional black colleges
teaching shakespeare and
aristotle

always without question
their votes are for demos
and their afros
have been transposed from
drip drip drip
to an inretrospect conk
called scary curl

they love martin on the
15th and the
4th

and think marcus g
is a little too fat
and loud for a jamaican

for about 28 days in february
they become engrossed
in themselves
and start to tell children
about that major historical
no no work entitled
"jamestown and the tarzan 20"

malcolm is a type of glasses
to wear
and kwanzaa
like streaking and yo-yos
departed their lives
with the calendar of their
choice

neo negro plays
new i-spy without
cosby complaints
and can't decide who is right
in angola
mozambique
and
eritrea

neo is transformed completion
of buppie-istic
post dashiki-ism
gravitating towards ultimate
confusion in the major
stage production of

"my fair negro"

it is presently on an unlimited
run at the
theatre
of
assimilation

negro infancy

when negroes realize that spoon feeding
is dependency,
their bibs will be cleaned of mush

for matriarchal fatherhood
is pampering while infants are helpless,

 the training must be channeled for

 breakaway.

grown men are assertive,
no one raises their high chairs
or simulacs their anger,

now
negroes are babies,
pacified mouths of unresponsive weakness
and misguided savagery tamed
in a simulated crib of confusion

when they grow and learn the
ancient techniques,

they will breast feed their own.

blaming victims

the need for upliftment regardless
of its nature is essential to the soul,
black men rely on black women for that.

the dried veil of crusted mascara is a
perversion of sexual misconduct complete with
black eyed mommas and split lip sisters —

"lemme smack me a bitch and get an erection!"

wrongness is a sociological mud pack
oozing into a soggy grouping of irresponsible
images on tv's, textbooks, and chalkboards

in between the cries from mutilated self esteems,
the rogue washes away like talc
and answers a faint call from misguided leaders
for the whichaways and whytheydo's.

it is now proven without a doubt —
a show called

"HOW TO RAPE A PEOPLE UNSUSPECTINGLY"

is number 1 on Nielsen.

the chocolate city poem #1
(upon mikhail's visit)

where it is darkest
it is whitest
america always lets the
shadows know that they are
only reflections of larger life.

around the corner from georgie
it is dark and scary
it is scary by massa's house
and it ain't on the moscow news.

when world leaders visit
the city rents the heat grates
out to the frozen wind

people even have to pay to freeze
to death in chocolate city
these days.

big mac or vodka

in el salvador they
sell truckloads
of big macs at the
newly built mcdonalds
they add tomato sauce
and cheese to the burgers
to make them taste
like pupusas*

govt leaders stay
sick with indigestion
doctors say there is too
much fat and beef in their
diets
stay away from big macs

many salvadoreans
hate big macs
they hide in the hills
drinking vodka and speak
of burning down the
mcdonalds
they are told that if
they hate big macs
so much
try the fish sandwiches
it is easier
on the stomach

the men in the hills are too
busy to eat
they spend their time
mixing cocktails
every day they come down from

the mountains to blow
up the mcdonalds and build a
liquor store to sell vodka
govt men make them leave
before they throw their cocktails
and start a riot

the president plans to build
a burger king across
from the mcdonalds
it will serve whoppers
for the people and
vodka for the men
who hide in the hills

it is said this won't
work either
he should tear down
the mcdonalds and build
a night club that serves
only pupusas

*pupusas - Salvador's most popular dish, consisting of tortilla, cheese, tomato sauce, meat, etc.

Revenge is as Sweet as Saki #2

Ever took a good look at
your
VCR
your
CD
your
TV?

Ever looked closely at your radios
wondered
Who owns the Earth
Who owns America?

Last night I dreamed
I met a woman named
ENOLA GAY
We made love in the back seat
of my '45 Toyota
Afterwards I looked at the back of
my radio and there were names I couldn't
pronounce
The McDonald's down the street was selling
sushi and saki
and Dan Rather was doing the news in more than
one language

Enola laughed and told me

> There are modern wars being fought
> on assembly lines and at bank counters
> and the way you catch a rat is to learn
> to run thru alleys

This morning I sold my Toyota and bought a pistol
The handle was engraved

MADE IN HIROSHIMA

america and the ant message
(for Amiri Baraka)

maybe ants are too deliberate.
               too conformist.
               too obedient.
               too organized.

and maybe ants are too much like the
military,
         too much like
         those guys in
         orwell's 1984
         under the rule
   of
   the

   thought
         police. (God forbid that.)

and maybe, just maybe
ants are too un-american,
because
         you can't eat steak everyday
         if you constantly think of
         all the others.

when i was younger,
i would marvel at their order,
how they collected crackers
calmly,
how they re-built their destroyed homes
after young "uncivilized" maniacs
stepped on their civilization
for cheap laughs.

but still,
ants just seem too refined
for
america,
seem too unalarmed,
too civilized.

then again,
i haven't ever seen an ant
beg for money or sleep on
a heat grate.

images of nelson

the flash of his weather beaten blackness
chills my bones like
cold rain in October,
>   droplets of time
>   connecting wrinkles
>   of pride with
>   the epidermis of
>   infinite struggle:

>   "until we are free,"
>   it says
>   "until we are free."

spatial eyes rotate solidarity into patronage,
determination spreads pure afrikan love

lips lilt freedom in a slumbering florescent
fog emerging allegiance into the
re-affirmation of his incessance

the face ranges perpetual service
guided by essential images,
the canvas glows commitment,
circling the globe with devotion
and the strength of an ageless magnetism
that is transcendentally immortal.

native son

        richard wright is the consummate
                alien.

he has no friends.
                no brothers   no sisters
                no children.
richard landed in 1940 on a spaceship
in chicago   he was arrested and jailed.
put in
        solitary.

richard has been a mystery ever since.

it was said he ate beef and vegetables,
drank liquor with reds,
killed two women in a panic, and hid
out in the snow.   when he was caught
he confessed about his
        "alienism"
        so

                they gave him a huge
                empty cell all to himself,
                sent him no visitors,
                gave him no mail.

                he was denied use of
                a telephone,
                and was shackled with
                huge weighted balls
                to drag around his cell

    for

eternity.

he is a strange guy this richard?

in 1982   they think another one landed.   alice.
she wrote strange little letters to GOD and they
made a movie about her getting in these arguments
with this guy who hated all women in the world
except one.   she was thrown in jail too.   the cell
next to richard.   only thing,   she is allowed a

"visitor"

and mail too.

somebody named...   toni.

i wonder how richard feels about this?

underground music scene
(for richard wright)

richard wright
  escaped from prison and became a
    reggae singer named
      cross damon,
        i saw him
          at a club on
            florida ave
              wearing dreadlocks
              smoking ganja
                and singing with
                  a group of
                    reed players
                      named
  ishmael.

broken pencils

james baldwin has always been dead.
held the funeral before jimmy
was even born.
held it on college campuses,
high schools,
broadway,
press rooms,
publishing houses,
printing companies,

one huge burial for
10 million invisible fingers
dead from writer's cramp.

you see awhile ago
this guy shot jimmy b,
shot jimmy b & sonia s,
amiri b & maya a,
june j & haki m,
gwendolyn b & ethelbert m,

shot them all in the back while
their granddadies wrote down
little verses down by the creek
for them to read when they grew up,
shot them all & tossed broken
pencils in the creek until
little black boys &
girls got lead poisoning in the brain
from drinking creek water.

after the funeral
they buried them all together
in a bunch,

all of our smoke kings and manchilds,
homegirls and sulas,
sonny's blues singers
and caged bird crooners.

all piled up in one big grave
with a million others
& a giant epitaph reading

"RICHARD AIN'T WRIGHT...
BIGGER KILLED MARY..."

ALSO AVAILABLE FROM THIRD WORLD PRESS

<u>Nonfiction</u>

The Destruction Of Black Civilization:
by Dr. Chancellor Williams
$16.95 (paper)
$29.95 (cloth)

The Cultural Unity Of Black Africa
by Cheikh Anta Diop
$14.95

Confusion By Any Other Name: The Negative Impact of The BlackMan's Guide to Understanding the Black-Woman
edited by Haki Madhubuti
$3.95

Home Is A Dirty Street : The Social Oppression of Black Children
by Useni Eugene Perkins
$9.95

The Isis Papers: The Keys to the Colors
by Dr. Frances Cress Welsing
$14.95 (paper)
$29.95 (cloth)

Reconstructing Memory: Black Literary Criticism
by Fred L. Hord
$12.95

Black Men: Obsolete, Single, Dangerous?
by Haki R. Madhubuti
$14.95 (paper)
$29.95 (cloth)

From Plan To Planet Life Studies: The Need For Afrikan Minds And Institutions
by Haki R. Madhubuti
$7.95

Enemies: The Clash Of Races
by Haki R. Madhubuti
$12.95

Kwanzaa: A Progressive And Uplifting African-American Holiday
Introduction by
Haki R. Madhubuti $2.50

A Move Further South
by Ruth Garnett
$7.95

Manish
by Alfred Woods
$8.00

New Plays for the Black Theatre (Anthology)
edited by Woodie King, Jr.
$14.95

Wings Will Not Be Broken
Darryl Holmes
$8.00

Jiva Telling Rites
Estella Conwill Majozo
$8.00

Sortilege (Black Mystery)
by Abdias do Nascimento
$2.95

Manish
by Alfred Woods
$8.00

Children's Books

The Day They Stole The Letter J
by Jabari Mahiri
$3.95

The Tiger Who Wore White Gloves
by Gwendolyn Brooks
$6.95

A Sound Investment
by Sonia Sanchez
$2.95

Afrocentric Self Inventory and Discovery Workbook
by Useni Perkins
$5.95

I Look At Me
by Mari Evans
$2.50

The Story of Kwanzaa
by Safisha Madhubuti
$5.95

The Brass Bed and Other Stories
Pearl Cleage
$8.00

The Future and Other Stories
by Ralph Cheo Thurmon
$8.00

Poetry and Drama

Blacks
by Gwendolyn Brooks
$19.95 (paper)
$35.95 (cloth)

To Disembark
by Gwendolyn Brooks
$6.95

I've Been A Woman
by Sonia Sanchez
$7.95

My One Good Nerve
by Ruby Dee
$8.95

Geechies
by Gregory Millard
$5.95

Earthquakes And Sunrise Missions
by Haki R. Madhubuti
$8.95

So Far, So Good
by Gil-Scott Heron
$8.00

Killing Memory: Seeking Ancestors
(Lotus Press)
by Haki R. Madhubuti
$8.00

Say That The River Turns: The Impact Of Gwendolyn Brooks
(Anthology)
Ed.by Haki R. Madhubuti
$8.95

Octavia And Other Poems
by Naomi Long Madgett
$8.00

Black BooksBulletin

Black Books Bulletin 1991 Annual
$15.00
A landmark issue marking the return of this important journal. Includes the work of Gwendolyn Brooks, Haki R. Madhubuti, Darwin Turner, Pearl Cleage, Conrid Worrill, Maulana Karenga, Robert Williams, Frances Cress Welsing and many others.

Back issues

A limited number of back issues of this unique journal are available at $3.00 each:
1)*Vol. 1, Fall '71*
Interview with Hoyt W. Fuller
2)*Vol. 1, No. 3*
Interview with
Lerone Bennett, Jr.
3)*Vol. 5, No. 3*
Science & Struggle
4)*Vol. 5, No. 4*
Blacks & Jews
5)*Vol. 7, No. 3*
The South

Third World Press books are available from your local bookstore or by mail from **Third World Press,** 7524 S. Cottage Grove Ave. Chicago, IL 60619. Ask for our complete catalog. Shipping: Add $2.50 for first book and .50 for each additional book. Mastercard/Visa orders may be placed by calling 1(312) 651-0700.